DATE DUE

OCT 17 1996			

D1021561

LAUGH KILLS LONESOME

&

other poems

MIKE LOGAN

Illustrations by Mike Korn

Additional copies of *Laugh Kills Lonesome* are available by sending $6.95 plus $1.50 postage and handling to:

Buglin' Bull Press
32 S. Howie, Helena, MT 59601

Buglin' Bull Press

32 S. Howie, Helena, MT 59601

Dedication

This book is dedicated to my brothers, Jim, Phil,
Jerry, and John and to my sister Debbie.
It is said that you can choose your friends,
but not your family. I would have chosen each
of them, as friends or family.

Foreword

In the foreword to Mike Logan's *Bronc to Breakfast*, Wally McRae dubs him a master craftsman and storyteller. That pair of top-hand qualities is more than what most cowboy poets pack as they shake their faces for their first chutegates—as they spur out their first books of verses.

Laugh Kills Lonesome is Mike's second book, however, and we, as readers, have the right to expect an even stronger lick—something "new and improved." And, by God, that's exactly what you'll find gracing the following pages.

Though it seems hardly possible, there's a more adventurous imagination working behind these poems, as evidenced by the witty and alliterative "Gaggles 'n Gangs, McCartys 'n Hangs":

> If turtles, they all crawl in "bales"
> And apes, they're called a "shrewdness,"
> Could a crew of drunken cowhands
> Be labeled as a *crudeness*?

As well as a much richer diction and keener image, such as that loping through the poem "Temptation":

> 'Til your horse kicks up an arrowhead
> Down near the bison kill
> Or he tries the road that swings around
> The old bootlegger's still.

And, to boot, genuine humor—the kind sparked by that fine-focused, *you-bet*-I've-been-there detail, highlighted in the poem "Ranch Truck":

> Hayhooks festoon the gearshift.
> There's stockwhips on the seat.
> Ol' Skipper's on the towchains
> That's piled beneath my feet.

Perhaps Mike Logan's greatest gift to his readers, however, is his uncanny knack for capturing historical facts, embellished with just the right pinch of drama and/or myth, in a way that permits us, a century later, to ride through the picture—*Lonesome Dove* style! Of the same grand vintage as his earlier piece, "The Wolf Creek Stage," here he gives us "Laugh Kills Lonesome," the title poem, and "Behold A Pale Horse," which very well could be Mike's most powerful writing to date.

This is all to say that if *Bronc To Breakfast* quirted your ticker from a walk into a trot, then *Laugh Kills Lonesome*—you can bet your riggin' sack, your favorite cowdog, AND THE RANCH—will spur your heart into a full gallop. These well-crafted, emotionally honest poems, along with Mike Korn's fancy-filigreed, silver-conchoed sketches riding shotgun, should make old Mike Logan and young Kid Russell both proud.

Paul Zarzyski

Introduction

Charlie Russell's *Laugh Kills Lonesome* touches me as no other painting does. To me, it is the saddest of all his works. He painted it the year before he died. Charlie loved that time when the wind truly did blow, unfettered, from Montana's Milk River to Mexico. He mourned its passing.

The poems in this book were written for fun or because something struck a chord deep inside me. They were not written as a book. "Gatherings" could well have been dedicated to my fellow cowboy poets. It was written with tongue in cheek. No other group I have ever been associated with complains less and supports each other more. I think it's because we don't compete, we gather, "just to have some fun" and to share our poems.

My thanks, once again, to Mike Korn for "riding shotgun" for me, as Paul Zarzyski puts it in the foreword, with his great illustrations and his equally valued advice.

A special thanks to Paul Zarzyski, for writing the foreword. The caption under a picture of Paul, in a recent issue of *Western Horseman,* proclaims that he "may be the best free-verse cowboy poet alive." In my opinion, Paul Zarzyski is one of the best and most dedicated poets of any kind in the country today. I am not alone in that opinion.

Thanks also to Bob Scriver, Liz Dear, Les Graham, Tuffy Cooper, and Wally McRae for the kind words on the back of this book. Each of these people is a treasure in his, or her, own right.

Bob Scriver has long been recognized as a national art treasure. Liz Dear is one of the founders of The Cowboy Poetry Gathering in Elko, Nevada. Les Graham and Tuffy Cooper are guardians of our nation's livestock industry and the heritage that goes along with it. Wally McRae was officially declared a national treasure, in September of 1990, when he received the National Heritage Award.

The old "Ranch Truck" is gone now, burned to a cinder in a freak fire. I forgot to ask Bruce and Fred Benson or their wives Pauline and Dot if they were able to salvage the "one old work horse shoe" or the "pair of ancient channel locks" or the "Swede saw." I know the "eight cents in cold hard cash" were long gone. I also know we'll never get a new "Ranch Truck" broke to drive quite as well. Maybe if we tried Runnin' W's . . .

Mike Logan
Helena, Montana 1990

Contents

Laugh Kills Lonesome

He called it LAUGH KILLS LONESOME.
Shows old friends around the fire
An' them boys is swappin' windys
Long before they savvied wire.

Charlie stands there in the firelight.
He's the nighthawk who's rode in.
He, mostly, talked to hosses.
Sang nightsongs to the wind.

That paintin' shows another time
When men rode all alone
An' yarnin' by the cookfire
Made a wagon seem like home.

You can feel ol' Charlie mournin'.
He'd 'a give up wealth an' fame
To ride back down them old trails
Before the land was tame.

LAUGH KILLS LONESOME, Charlie loved it,
That time now long ago,
When the wind still blew, unfettered,
From the Milk to Mexico.

Romantic

"Now, ranch life's plumb romantic!"
I heard this jaybird say
As he graced the drugstore counter.
It was fifty five that day.

He was wearin' purty feathers
In his big ol' cowboy hat
An' his face was smooth as butter
Or the cream you feed the cat.

"Yep, ranch life it's romantic!"
He took another sip
Of his new Swiss Mocha coffee
An' I think he burnt his lip.

I was buyin' some more ointment
For the frostbite on my cheek
An' I saw the wind a turnin'
As I listened t' this geek.

Ain't nothin' much romantic
When it's forty five below
An' the wind's a toppin' fifty
An' a pilin' up the snow.

When yer beard 'n face's freezin'
An' yer pitchin' loads of hay
Off the stacks you built with beaverslides
One fiery summer's day.

Ain't nothin' much romantic
When the Farm Hand it won't go
An' you gotta pitch the haysled full
At forty five below.

When the big teams is a steamin'
As they pull the heavy sled
Through the cattle that's all humped up
An' a waitin' t' be fed.

Ain't nothin' much romantic
When that damn wind cuts t' bone,
When yer out there choppin' water
An' yer hands has turned t' stone.

When the temp'ature an' wind chill
Is a trav'lin' in cahoots
An' yer feet's two lumps of hoarfrost
Even in yer felt lined boots.

Ain't nothin' much romantic
When the hosses go sharp shod
An' you see the mad dog faces
Of the howlin' winter god.

When there's ice from all the meltin'
After yesterday's chinook
'Cause the merc'ry's dropped a hundred points.
A half day's all it took.

Ain't nothin' much romantic
When you start the day with dread,
'Cause you know out in the open
Any calves is freezin' dead.

"Yep, ranch life it's romantic."
I heard this jaybird say
As he graced the drugstore counter.
It was fifty five that day.

There Was a Time

There was a time when handshakes
Meant more 'n a contract now.
When if you gave a man your hand
You took a solemn vow.

There was a time when justice
Meant more 'n just playin' a game.
When guilty men weren't turned loose
To rob and kill and maim.

There was a time when marriage
Meant more 'n just sayin' "I do."
When man and wife were mates for life
And worked the tough times through.

There was a time when manners
Meant more 'n just "thanks" and "please."
When men could rise or hold the door
And not feel ill at ease.

There was a time when freedom
Meant more 'n just "What's for me?"
When each right carried with it
Responsibility.

There was a time when fam'lies
Meant more 'n just groups hard pressed.
When mothers still taught daughters
And fathers still knew best.

There was a time when learnin'
Meant more 'n just what's in school.
When neighbors helped each other
And we lived the golden rule.

There was a time when American
Meant strong and proud and free.
When people's thoughts weren't molded
By that wasteland on TV.

There was a time, there was a time.
That time could come again
If wisdom, love and honor
Would rule the hearts of men.

When Tommie Turned the Wolf Loose

Ol' Tom, he's turned the wolf loose.
He's set t' howl 'til dawn.
He's dancin' with them purty girls
An' drinkin' "who hit John."

Before he starts this ball t' roll,
Ol' Tommie he bathed twice
Then took a shave an' haircut
An' got dressed up real nice.

So when he hits The Longbranch,
Tom's feelin' quite the gent.
He's got his whole year's bankroll
An' plans to see it spent.

He loses some a playin' stud,
But cards ain't his long suit,
Just tells the barkeep, "Set 'em up,
'Cause it's my night to hoot."

He tries the wheel a time or two.
His luck it runs plumb cold,
But that don't slow our Tommie none.
He still feels mighty bold.

His roll, it starts t' dwindle some,
But he keeps buyin' drinks.
His fancy duds is wrinklin' fast,
But ol' Tom never blinks.

Them cactus squeezin's brave Tom up
An' he goes on the fight.
Claims he's the toughest man in town.
His talk's some impolite.

One puncher, he don't want no fight,
But Tom heaps on abuse
'Til sudden like this feller
Turns 'im ever' way but loose.

Tom's strategy's plumb brilliant.
He'll slow this cowhand's pace.
He's blockin' all them punches
With the front parts of his face.

Tom's next plan's even brillianter.
He's wearin' his victim down.
Boy purt' near breaks both boot heels.
On the "toughest man in town."

His final play's sheer genius.
That ranny's arms is sore
From takin' Tom to pitch 'im through
That left hand swingin' door.

His nose is broke an' two teeth's gone.
His left eye's got this twitch.
His rope hand feels plumb busted
An' he's face down in the ditch.

His right hind leg don't track just right.
Both ears is cropped real good.
His jaw sits catywampus.
Don't work just like it should.

Yep, Tom he's turned the wolf loose.
By damn, but this's fun.
Cain't hardly wait til next year's ball
Right after shippin's done.

Wrecks

Well, I've seen some wrecks ahorseback
An' quite a few with cars,
An' I've even seen the carnage
Of some awful wrecks in bars.

But the worst wrecks in my mem'ry
Was the ones a comin' on
When there come a perfumed letter
That started off "Dear John."

Colors

This feller from a magazine
Was askin' Booger Bill
About his life ahorseback,
The way such fellers will.

"What was your fav'rite color horse
And can you tell me why?"
Ol' Booger cogitated some
An' this was his reply.

"I've knowed some men rode only blacks
Or buckskins or a paint
Or browns or appaloosies.
That particular, I ain't.

I've knowed a few that leaned towards roans
An' others towards a bay
An' lots o' hands like sorrels,
But I guess I'd have to say

I've rode a lot of each shade
An', while it maybe should,
His color never mattered
If the hoss I rode was good."

Gatherings

Well, there's gatherings of eagles
And of cowboy poets, too.
Now, mostly, eagles don't complain,
But cowboy poets do.

They complain if they're not featured
Or, sometimes, if they are.
They complain about the weather
And the cost of their new car.

They complain about the planning
And how the show is run.
They complain, if they was ramrod
They'd show 'em how it's done.

They complain about folklorists
And all academicians.
They complain about the stagelights
And damnable musicians.

They complain about the poems
That their fellow poets say.
They complain about the distance
That they had to drive that day.

They complain about the shortness
Of their time up on the stage.
And a few of them have even voiced
Complaints about old age.

They complain about motel rooms
Or the campin' place they got.
They complain that fame ain't found 'em
That ol' Wally ain't so hot.

They complain they ain't seen Elko
Or the Johnny Carson show.
And they complain that those that has
No way deserved to go.

They complain about the whiskey
Or the prices in the store.
They complain, complain, complain, complain
And then complain some more.

Now *my* complaint with gatherings
And all those woes and sighs,
Is that all of us complainers
Is really such nice guys.

Well, maybe we've all lost the trail,
'Cause reason number one
That we all come to gatherings
Is just to have some fun.

I Shot Jim Dance This Mornin'

I shot Jim Dance this mornin'.
Like a dog wolf, don't ya see.
Shot 'im with my ol' Sharps rifle.
Now I'm hangin' from this tree.

Don't think that I'm complainin',
'Cause I'd do it all again.
What he done to my Sweet Lisa
Was a pure an' mortal sin.

I shot Jim Dance this mornin'.
He was ridin' out 'o town.
I was happy that I shot 'im.
Lord, I wish they'd cut me down.

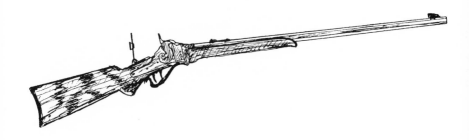

Don't think that I'm complainin'.
I was hung with this new rope,
But I sent Jim Dance to Hades.
'Least that's my fondest hope.

I shot Jim Dance this mornin'
'Neath the palin' of the moon.
Now I'm dancin' here on thin air,
'Cause they hung me at high noon.

Don't think that I'm complainin',
'Cause I watched Sweet Lisa die
After Jim Dance went and stabbed her.
Lord, I couldn't even cry.

I shot Jim Dance this mornin'.
Shot 'im dead right in his track.
Just ran an' grabbed my ol' Sharps
An' shot 'im in the back.

Don't think that I'm complainin'.
Jim Dance'll burn in Hell,
And I'll be with Sweet Lisa
Where all the angels dwell.

Reflections in a Dentist's Chair

I'm sittin' here, white knuckled,
In this modern dentist's chair.
They're treatin' me plumb gentle
With lots of lovin' care.

Ain't felt the slightest hint of pain.
Cain't hardly hear them drills.
They're playin' me soft music.
I'm doped up t' the gills.

This contoured seat's so comf'terble
I'm driftin' back in time.
I'll think of saddle hosses
An' old time trails t' climb.

I always wished that I was born
Way back in olden days.
The West was wild 'n wooly then
An' men weren't popinjays.

I prob'ly would 'a partnered up
With Bridger 'n them boys
'A fightin' griz 'n Blackfeet
An' learnin' nature's joys.

Or maybe I'd 'a moiled for gold,
Out there in 'forty nine,
When nuggets was as thick as fleas
An' weren't no need t' mine.

I wish I could 'a rode them trails
A hunderd years ago
T' help 'em bring them cow herds up
From down by Mexico.

I might 'a rode the owl hoot trail
When Butch 'n Sundance did
'A carvin' notches in m' gun
An' bein' called "The Kid."

Or maybe I'd 'a joined that charge
That some folks thought insane,
Ol' Teddy led up San Juan Hill
T' help avenge the "Maine."

But these is all reflections
In this modern dentist's chair.
They're treatin' me plumb gentle,
With lots of lovin' care

An', deep down in my heart, I know
It wouldn't 'a worked nohow
'Cause I savvy old time dentists
Would 'a made me wish for now.

Oh, I might 'a fought them Blackfeet
An' treated griz some rough,
But for an old time dentist,
I ain't near tough enough.

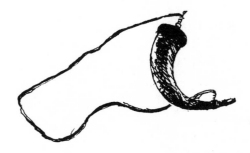

Peace and Health

May the God who gave us Christmas,
When His only son was born,
Bless you, your friends and family
On this Holy Christmas Morn.

May he give you all fat cattle
And your best rope horse to ride.
May your trails lead through a New Year
Where peace and health abide.

Deep January

The sun is cold.
The old god's here.
He names this month
That starts the year.

The sun is cold
And earth lies dead
When Janus walks
With numbing tread.

The sun is cold.
The morning stills.
Deep winter stalks
Snow covered hills.

The sun is cold
And spectral trees,
Bare limbed and gaunt,
Just stand and freeze.

The sun is cold
And rivers deep,
'Neath thick blue ice,
Enshroud their sleep.

The sun, no more,
Will warm the day
'Til Janus ends
His icebound sway.

Temptation

You think you know temptation
'Cause you've seen the city lights
Or the gleam of easy money
Or some dance hall girls in tights?

You think you know temptation?
Well, boys, I'm tellin' you,
'Til you've rode a horse to school in spring,
You haven't got a clue.

'Til you've seen the breaks a greenin'
An' the days is warmin' up
An' you're ten years old, ahorseback,
Followed by your fav'rite pup.

'Til the meadowlarks is singin'
An' a leadin' you both on
An' the dandylion's is bloomin'
By a newborn whitetail fawn.

'Til you know there's lessons waitin'
In the schoolhouse just for you,
But the crick's a siren callin'
An' the sky's its deepest blue.

'Til you see a pair of greenwings
Or a baby cottontail
Or a killdeer fakes a broken wing
To lead you off the trail.

'Til your horse kicks up an arrowhead,
Down near the bison kill,
Or he tries the road that swings around
The old bootlegger's still.

'Til your pup's a chasin' butterflies
Or huns up in the draw
Or a work horse colt comes wobblin' up,
On new legs, with his ma.

'Til the sage hens is a struttin'
On the hill beside the school
An' the thought of learnin' hist'ry
Seems a fate unjust an' cruel.

Now them is real temptations,
Not like the lust for gold
Or the mad desire for power
That can seize you when you're old.

You think you know temptation?
Well, boys, I'm tellin' you,
'Til you've rode a horse to school in spring,
You haven't got a clue.

Missouri Lost

Broad shouldered at its birthplace
In sight of the Spanish Peaks.
Child of three rolling rivers
And a thousand singing creeks.

The wild Missouri flowed to the north
In a swift free watered arc,
Through mountain gates to the prairies
Great bison herds turned dark.

Its great falls thundered high and free
Through rainbow misted air.
Their foaming trout-filled waters
Fed the eagle and the "great white bear."

Its draws hid the stalk of the buffalo wolf
As he culled the weak and the old.
Then sang primeval wolf songs
To a full moon blue and cold.

Its shores felt the prance of the war horse
As he waited for the raid to begin.
They quavered at the fearsome war cries
When he carried his warrior in.

Its banks knew the tread of an Indian maid
And two captains who hoped there'd be,
At the source of this storied river,
A passage to the Northwest Sea.

Its currents felt the waddle of the bullboat
And the keelboat with plews in the hold.
They parted at the surge of the paddlewheel
Bringing miners in their quest for gold.

Its breaks, long ago, harbored bighorn sheep
Of a kind that is known no more.
They echoed when bull elk bugled at the moon
As the trees turned to gold on the shore.

Its waters slaked the thirst of Texas cows
As drovers pushed them north
In search of grass that stretched to the sky
Where war parties once set forth.

Its cottonwoods fed the branding fires
Where the cow thief plied his trade.
They served as the grisly hanging trees
When the rustler's debt was paid.

Its hills sprouted high stone monuments
When the sheepherder's wooly flocks
Were welcomed to the cowman's country
Like a siege of some deadly pox.

Its torrents carried off the thin topsoil
As homesteaders came, with the plow,
To carve up the virgin high plains
And fence out the longhorn cow.

Its lifeblood gushed through new cut veins
Where the white man built his store
And irrigated the benchlands
And washed the miner's ore.

That wild Missouri is harnessed now,
Like some docile plodding ox.
No longer a plunging red horned bull,
It is yoked by the concrete box.

No great falls thunder free, today.
No wolf songs fill the air
And the west wind keening down the Great Divide
Mourns the passing of the "great white bear."

If you listen some dark, quiet night,
You can still feel the ancient beast
As he tests the strength of his concrete cage
Then growls away to the east.

Broad shouldered at its birthplace
In sight of the Spanish Peaks.
Child of three rolling rivers
And a thousand singing creeks.

Lullaby

I've heard "Ave Marias"
In cathedrals spired and tall,
And I've heard orchestral thunder
Fill a great symphonic hall.

I've heard celestial concerts
Sung by tabernacle choirs,
And I've heard great Verdi operas
With the awe that each inspires.

I've heard the joyous wedding march
As couples said their vows,
And I've heard the calming smoothness
Of a nightherd's song to cows.

I've heard the haunting harmonies
Of mouth harps played alone,
And I've heard the plaint of lovesongs
Sad enough to melt a stone.

I've heard the skirl of bagpipes
On a far flung battlefield,
And I've heard John Philip Sousa played
As nations' fates were sealed.

But the sweetest sound of music,
For me, will always be
The simple Irish lullaby
My mother sang to me.

Earthbound

One morning, against a crystal sky,
I watched the flight of a swan.
A graceful white winged line, he flew
At the edge of a rose gold dawn.

He'd flown a path no compass knew
From the shores of some far flung sea.
His lonely, far skied, haunting call
Seemed a message just for me.

"Come, follow me," he seemed to say,
"Where the north wind never blows."
"Come, follow me to a distant land
That only the wild swan knows."

Earthbound I stood that rose gold dawn,
Feet planted in the frozen snow,
But I wished for wings that could carry me
To the place where the wild swans go.

When Horses Talk War
There's Small Chance for Peace

Charlie Russell left this tableau
Of the old time cow camp way
When men was up and saddled
Before the break of day.

This bronc's a makin' war talk.
Blowin' rollers t' the sky.
There ain't one sign of peaceful
In that ol' roan's wicked eye.

Ol' Bob's a standin' easy.
While he ain't bent on war,
Way he's holdin' that McCarty tells
They've had this talk before.

He's workin' on his mornin' smoke.
His fish is tied plumb loose.
Ain't makin' one concession
T' no cold backed roan cayuse.

The roan's all bunched an' goosey.
He's proddy 'n some tough.
His medicine's plumb potent
An' his war talk ain't no bluff.

First light it's just a showin'.
Dawn's comin' cold an' damp.
Looks like ol' Bob an' Roanie's
Gonna entertain the camp.

Daughter of the Moon

Daughter of the moon, she was.
Killer come in soundless flight.
List'ner of the silent forest.
Flyer of the cold blue night.

Now she sits in blazing sunlight.
Blind, the world she still defies.
Wingbroke in the deep snowed fencerow.
Fierce, she blinks huge yellow eyes.

In on jet black wings to taunt her,
Queen who'd ruled the woodland gloom,
Wing the raucous kill voiced magpies.
Proud, she stands to face her doom.

Gaggles 'n Gangs, McCartys 'n Hangs

We had a vis'tor at the ranch,
This gent he was a "Limey,"
And the names he gave t' critters,
They sounded plumb old timey.

He said turkeys roam in "rafters"
And pheasants in "bouquets"
And larks in "exaltations,"
While squirrels, they climb in "drays."

"If you look where these names come from,"
Said he, "You're sure to see
What, in fifteenth century England,
They called 'Books of Courtesy'."

"They tried to give each group of beasts
A proper nomenclature,
That's socially acceptable,
When one discusses nature."

Now when his lordship took his leave,
I thought I'd try my hand
At givin' bunches on the range
Some names we'd understand.

If geese all glide in "gaggles"
And elk, they graze in "gangs,"
Do you think it might be possible
That rustlers swung in *hangs*?

And if fish all swim in "schools"
And dogs, they run in "packs,"
Would you think it plumb surprisin'
If saddles bunched in *kacks*?

If moles all dig in "labors"
And jays, they form a "party,"
Do you s'pose a bunch of lead ropes
Might braid up a *McCarty*?

If you hear a "charm" of finches
Or a "parliament" of owls
Is there any way that families
Of coyotes could be *howls*?

If you see some swine in "sounders"
Could broncs, they fight in *bucks*
Or groups of irrigators
Go out to work in *mucks*?

If you find a "knot" of hoptoads
Or a plover "congregation,"
Could roosts of trouble makin' crows
Be dubbed an *aggravation*?

If turtles, they all crawl in "bales"
And apes, they're called a "shrewdness,"
Could a crew of drunken cowhands
Be labeled as a *crudeness*?

Could polecats waft in *pungencies*
Or sheep get trimmed in *shears*
Or rock chucks feed in *munches*
Or wolves, they hunt in *weres*?

Could lambs, they go in *gambols*
Or cougars slink in *prowls*
Or bees all buzz in *bumbles*
Or spurs hang up in *rowels*?

Could heifers turn *Houdinis*
As they slip between the wires
Or punchers slouch in *windies*
When they're yarnin' 'round the fires?

Could hawks, they mouse in *hovers*
Or bulls, they form a *beller*
Or magpies make a *mischief*
Or auctioneers a *seller*?

This word game's run away with me.
I'm plumb confused at times.
If cowboy poets, frosted up
Would they recite in *rimes*?

Well, friends, I think you get my drift.
This went from bad to worse.
'Sides I know them cowboy poets
Would rather form a *verse*.

When the
Bulls of Autumn Come

It is a time of magic.

A time when summer's green yields to the gentle alchemy of autumn and begins its annual melting into gold.

A time when dawn's first kiss is silvered by the hoarfrost.

A time when hatches rise to wink ephemeral wings against an Indian summer sun.

It is a time of magic when the bulls of autumn come.

Burial

Well, boys, you know ol' Moon 'n me
Was partnered up fer years.
I got to say a word 'r two
If I can fight the tears.

I know ol' Moon'll understand
If we make this some quick.
Them cows is run t' hell 'n gone
All up an' down this crick.

An', Boss, I'd take it kindly
If you could say the prayer.
Ol' Moon he thought the world of you.
Said you was always square.

An', Billie, when we're finished
Could you sing that old church tune?
You know the one, "Amazing Grace,"
It meant a lot to Moon.

Moon's gone an' crossed that last big range
An' left me here alone.
An' boys I don't mind tellin' you,
M' heart's plumb turned t' stone.

That lightnin' storm come up so quick
Moon didn't shed his gun.
I think the strike that killed 'im
Caused the cows to make the run.

Killed his hoss an' him together
In a great blue blindin' flash.
Them cows was up an' runnin'
'Fore we even heard the crash.

They just run 'im down t' ribbons
An' his hoss 'n saddle too.
An' ever' cow in that stompede
Clashed horns a glowin' blue.

St. Elmo danced his cold blue fire
On ever' longhorned head,
But 'fore I even seen 'em jump
I knowed ol' Moon was dead.

He come out from Kentucky
When he was just a kid.
He always had the makin's.
Usually claimed I never did.

Ol' Moon was plumb good natured.
Purt' near always wore a grin.
He seemed to hunt the good side
Of hosses, life 'n men.

If ol' Moon told you somethin'
You could bet your poke it's true.
He'd side you in a tight spot
An' prob'ly josh you through.

He plumb shore savvied hosses
An' he shore did know the cow.
If St. Pete's needin' top hands,
He's got one comin' now.

Well, Moon, we gotta gather cows.
I'm gonna miss you, Pard.
I know you'll have the latch string out
When I play my last card.

Don't play tricks on them angels,
Or, leastways don't get caught.
An' keep them makin's ready
An' the coffee good 'n hot.

Boss.

Oh, Lord, this man we're sendin's
The best we've got to give.
It's hard for us to see, right now,
Why ol' Moon couldn't live.

But, Lord, you know your business
An' when to send the word
An' who you need t' help you
When you're trailin' Heaven's herd.

I'd put Moon out there ridin' point.
There ain't no better hand.
I know he'll learn them trails of gold
Just like he knew this land.

Just give ol' Moon a string of broncs
An' please don't fence 'im in.
He's used to big skied ranges.
Well, thank you, Lord. Amen.

Billie.

"Amazing grace, how sweet the sound
That saved a wretch like me.
I once was lost, but now am found.
Was blind, but now I see."

Adios, compadre.

The Shaman's Hands

Ghost winds howl off the Great Divide
To shape the Blackfeet lands.
Their wild, free, sculpting symphonies
Inspired the shaman's hands.

This artist's hands and fertile mind,
Known through the world today,
Have captured, in patinaed bronze,
Lovesongs composed in clay.

They've sung of "No More Buffalo,"
Of old ways doomed to die,
Uncompromising fierceness in
A cowboy's "Honest Try."

These wondrous hands have wrought, for us,
Two captains and their men
And tiny, brave "Bird Woman"
Who came to be their friend.

They've spun us tales of mountain men
Who rode up trails unknown
To seek the wealth of beaver plews
In mountains hewn from stone.

This night, we join in homage,
Through all Montana's lands,
To Robert Macfie Scriver
And his mystic shaman's hands.

Written and said for Robert Macfie Scriver, recipient of the 1990 Governor's Award for Distinguished Achievement in the Arts, Saturday, February 3, 1990, Great Falls, Montana.

Behold a Pale Horse

"And I looked, and behold a pale horse: and his name that sat on him was Death, and Hell followed with him."

Revelations 6:8

Montana 1886
A pale horse first appears.
White shadow on a drought struck range.
The coldest fall in years.

That horse he first was sighted
Up north on Crooked Creek,
The day the year's worst storm blew in
And howled for more 'n a week.

He seemed some awful phantom.
Some harbinger of doom.
That pale horse lopin' cold and gaunt
Through winter's gatherin' gloom.

Most outfits wintered cows that year
That usu'lly they'd 'a sold,
'Cause cattle prices dropped so far
That cowmen chanced the cold.

He ghosted down the Musselshell
Behind a warm chinook.
Froze sheaths of ice on all the grass
With just his pale eyed look.

That horse loped towards the Judith
And filled that range with dread
'Cause, where he went, great blizzards struck
And whole cow herds lay dead.

He worked his evil 'cross the plains
And up the Little Dry.
Wreaked havoc as he passed that way.
More herds laid down to die.

It got to where, to cut his track
Filled cowmen's hearts with fear
As coulees clogged with starvin' cows
That grim and direful year.

Cowhands lost toes and fingers
As they fought to save their herds.
The sight of cattle dyin' slow
Was pain too fierce for words.

That horse's passin' iced the streams
And thirst crazed steers broke through
And drowned as others pushed 'em in.
Weren't nothin' Man could do.

When spring, it finally came that year
Old timers still take vows
That men could walk for miles and miles
On carcasses of cows.

The Hell that followed with that horse
Was in the eyes of men
Who'd rolled the dice with nature
And seen their life's dreams end.

They called it, The Hard Winter.
It blew the winds of change,
When Death he rode a pale horse
And killed the open range.

Which You Want to See

"North," he said, "I'm headin' north.
I hate the bugs and heat.
I don't like chiggers in my beard.
It's north I will retreat."

"South," he said, "I'm headin' south.
I hate this ice and snow.
I don't like hoarfrost in my beard.
It's south I want to go."

"East," he said, "I'm headin' east.
I hate this sage and dust.
I don't like 'skeeters in my beard.
It's east I'll go, or bust."

"West," he said, "I'm headin' west.
I hate huge crowds to see.
I don't like sea salt in my beard.
It's west I wish to be."

"South," I said, "You don't like south?
You hate both east and west?
You don't like northwind in your beard?
You'll find no place that's best."

"North," I said, "I'm headin' north.
I love the northern lights.
I'd like to trail the caribou
And fish through sun filled nights."

"South," I said, "I'm headin' south.
I love to hear that drawl.
I'd like to see the dogwood bloom
And hear a bobwhite call."

"East," I said, "I'm headin' east.
I love New England falls.
I'd like to walk through red gold leaves
And see the Hudson's walls."

"West," I said, "I'm headin' west.
I love the Great Divide.
I'd like to hunt the buglin' bulls
And find new trails to ride."

North and south and east and west,
We'd each been to them all,
But all the things that I'd seen good,
He'd noticed not at all.

What matters, then? It's not so much
The place where you might be.
It, more, depends on good and bad
And which you want to see.

If It Ain't Broke

There's a sayin' on the ranches
They don't know in Washingtown.
"If a thing ain't broke, don't fix it."
Seems they've got it turned around.

If the government finds somethin'
That's functionin' just right,
They'll, just natural, microscope it
'Til some problem comes to light.

Well, they'll study it an' poke it
An' write a grant or two.
When it's plumb eviscerated,
This is what they'll do.

They'll form a new bureaucracy
An' write an EIS
An' appoint three new committees
To sort out this awful mess.

They'll hire twenty city lawyers
An' a judge to go along.
Then check with all the protest groups
To see what they done wrong.

They'll hold ninety open hearings,
Spendin' fabulous amounts,
Then ignore all your ideas.
John Q. Rancher never counts.

They'll ask the house and senate
For a new fact findin' junket
To see if some new plan of theirs'll
Pass the test or flunk it.

They'll waste plenty million dollars
On this thing that used to work.
Then toss their mass of findings
In front of some young clerk.

They'll add multitudes of helpers
To be facilitators
An' for ever three or four of them,
Two new administrators.

They'll build a brand new headquarters
In Washingtown D.C.
An', if ever'thing goes just right,
Send reports to you an' me.

What's the moral of this story?
It really ain't no joke.
Don't ever tell the government
If what you got ain't broke.

Waitin' for a Chinook

Dear Louie,
You wrote an' asked me
How the cows was doin' this year.
I wish I had some good news,
But I got this picture here.

Kid Russell's wintered up with me.
He drawed this little card.
I think it purt' near tells the tale.
This winter's hit us hard.

You know you had five thousand
When the first snows hit last fall,
But 'cept fer one last starvin' cow
Dad Winter's got 'em all.

That one ol' cow's a standin' there,
Back humped against the snow.
Her ribs is showin' like a map.
Her head's a hangin' low.

She's last of all five thousand,
That one ol' dyin' cow.
Just waitin' for a warm chinook,
But it won't save 'er now.

Jesse

Ranch Truck

A ranch truck's like a rancher.
Don't dress up fit t' kill.
Just goes an' gets the job done
Without no pomp or frill.

While they ain't long on beauty,
Ranch trucks can hold their own.
Just see if this ol' pickup
Don't sound like some you've known.

Me an' Bruce hop in his pickup.
We got some hay to load.
He's got 'er chained on all four wheels
'Cause last night it shore snowed.

Hayhooks festoon the gearshift.
There's stockwhips on the seat.
Ol' Skipper's on the towchains
That's piled beneath my feet.

The windshield's cracked an' muddy.
I give ol' Skip a shove.
The dash wears thirteen mittens
An' one odd left-hand glove.

It also sports three hammers,
Two pairs of fencin' pliers,
A stick 'r two of kindlin'
From last spring's brandin' fires,

Five caps an' some old glasses,
A Pepsi can 'r two,
A box of mixed up nuts an' bolts
An' one old work horse shoe.

There's binder twine an' ear tags,
Some string wound on a spool,
A can of pills for calf scours
An' a new ear taggin' tool,

A shot r' two of Longicil,
A length of rawhide thong,
A pair of ancient channel locks,
A tape just ten feet long,

A crescent wrench, a pill gun,
Band aids, a chain saw file,
Three scarves an' one old down vest
All wadded in a pile,

Six washers on a twist of wire,
Eight cents in cold hard cash,
A clevis, a direction book,
An' that's just on the dash.

Between us there's two sacks of cake,
Three jackets an' some chaps,
A slicker an' a Swede saw
An' three new leadrope snaps.

The floor holds one old halter,
An ax, two pairs of spurs,
A head stall an' two oil cans
An' a blanket full of burrs,

Some gunny sacks, a brandin' iron,
A brand new ropin' rope,
A pair of irrigatin' boots
An' a bar of Lava soap.

No tellin' what's behind the seat.
I'm sure ol' Bruce cain't say,
But we won't worry 'bout what's there
'Cause it ain't in the way.

We lost a tally book last week.
I'm 'fraid we're out of luck.
It's prob'ly lost forever
In Bruce's ol' red truck.

Sounds like I'm knockin' Bruce's truck?
Well, that'd be plumb mean.
'Sides, we thought of usin' my rig,
But it ain't half that clean.

About the Author

PHOTO / JUDY LOGAN

Mike Logan's interest in photographing life on the ranches of Montana provides the basis for many of his poems. His first book of poetry was entitled *Bronc To Breakfast & other poems.*

Two books of color photography also wear Mike's brand, *Montana Is . . .* and *Yellowstone Is . . . .* His photographs and stories have appeared in numerous magazines, calendars and books.

A featured poet and emcee at The National Cowboy Poetry Gathering in Elko, Nevada, and at The Montana Cowboy Poetry Gathering in Big Timber, Montana, Mike has also been featured at various gatherings across Alberta, Saskatchewan and British Columbia.

About the Illustrator

PHOTO / MIKE LOGAN

Mike Korn is a multi-talented individual. Long-time folklorist for the state of Montana, he is a warehouse of knowledge about the folk ways of the West and of Montana. Mike is a gifted illustrator, writer, musician, speaker, leatherworker, and sometimes cowhand. Mike currently works for the Montana Department of Fish, Wildlife and Parks.

He lives near Helena with his wife Jane and twin daughters, Lauren and Alicia.

As one of the founders of The National Cowboy Poetry Gathering in Elko, Nevada, and The Montana Cowboy Poetry Gathering, Mike Korn has left permanent tracks across the West.